FRANCIS OF ASSISI

Author:
Justin Lang

Illustrations:
Miguel Berzosa

ST. ANTHONY MESSENGER PRESS
Cincinnati, Ohio

ÉDITIONS
DU SIGNE

AT THE END OF THE 12TH CENTURY, ASSISI WAS A THRIVING TOWN. ITS YOUNG PEOPLE ENJOYED LIFE.

Let's drink to our friend Francis since he just turned 18!

A toast to the happiest guy in Assisi!

Thanks! Cheers for wine, music and friends.

The love of my heart gives me wings...

3

Please, sir.

Here, take this! Enjoy yourself!

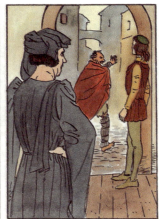

Francis, I forbid you to act like this! You take my hard-earned money and throw it out the window!

Calm down! You know that he isn't a bad young man.

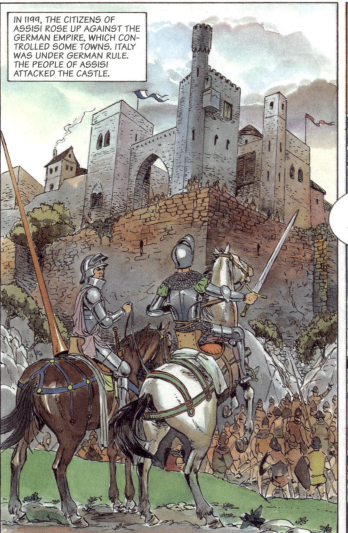

IN 1199, THE CITIZENS OF ASSISI ROSE UP AGAINST THE GERMAN EMPIRE, WHICH CONTROLLED SOME TOWNS. ITALY WAS UNDER GERMAN RULE. THE PEOPLE OF ASSISI ATTACKED THE CASTLE.

Have courage! Let's fight for our freedom!

THE PEOPLE OF ASSISI WON THE BATTLE AND TOOK CHARGE OF THEIR OWN TOWN AGAIN. THEY REBUILT ITS WALLS. THE NOBLES WHO WERE CONNECTED TO THE GERMANS HAD TO ESCAPE.

Do you think that I'd make a good knight?

You look like one.

You don't have the courage to use the sword...

Look, my friends! We're in danger of being attacked tomorrow...

FRANCIS BECAME RESTLESS. THINGS GOT BETTER FOR A WHILE, BUT IN 1202 A NEW WAR BROKE OUT. PERUGIA, A NEARBY TOWN, ATTACKED ASSISI. FRANCIS WAS TAKEN PRISONER.

With winter coming, there'll be even less food.

The days seem to drag...

What a life in this hole!

Take heart, men, take heart. The sun is still shining. Its light never dries up. Let's sing! The future belongs to us.

AFTER A YEAR, THE YOUNG BERNARDONE WAS RELEASED, BUT HE GOT SICK. AFTER A FEW WEEKS:

Do you feel better today?

The countryside is beautiful... At other times I would have enjoyed looking at it. But today it doesn't interest me. Why?

You have such a proud way of walking!

Well, no wonder! These clothes cost me a small fortune.

Yes, I'm going. But I'll have heroes to show me the way. Your son will be a great knight. I'll make the Bernardone family famous!

AFTER RECOVERING FROM HIS ILLNESS, FRANCIS DECIDED TO RETURN TO WAR.

A FEW DAYS LATER

You're a gentleman, aren't you? You don't want to go and fight in clothes like that!

Your new tailored suit? It's much too good for me!

FRANCIS FELT GOOD ABOUT WHAT HE HAD DONE. BUT HE STILL DIDN'T HAVE HIS OLD ENTHUSIASM. HE LEFT ASSISI WITH HIS SQUIRE TO GO TO SOUTHERN ITALY. BUT THE NEXT NIGHT:

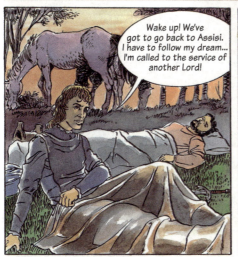

Wake up! We've got to go back to Assisi. I have to follow my dream... I'm called to the service of another Lord!

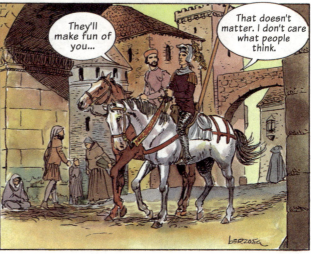

They'll make fun of you...

That doesn't matter. I don't care what people think.

berzosa

WHEN HE RETURNED TO ASSISI, FRANCIS AVOIDED PARTIES. HE LIKED TO GO INTO THE FOREST TO PRAY. HE ALSO GAVE AWAY EVERYTHING HE OWNED.

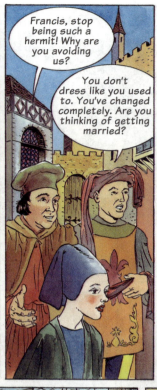

Francis, stop being such a hermit! Why are you avoiding us?

You don't dress like you used to. You've changed completely. Are you thinking of getting married?

The one to whom I will pledge my life is so wonderful, so beautiful and so awesome that you can't even imagine it!

WHO WAS HE TALKING ABOUT?

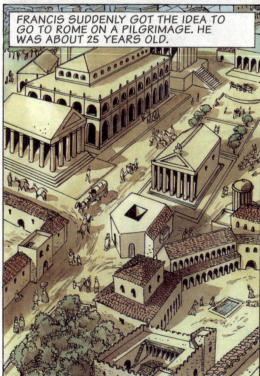

FRANCIS SUDDENLY GOT THE IDEA TO GO TO ROME ON A PILGRIMAGE. HE WAS ABOUT 25 YEARS OLD.

Let's exchange clothes!

THE BEGGAR WAS AMAZED AT FRANCIS.

Aren't you embarrassed to wear those rags?

No. I'm glad to. I've found the love of my life: Lady Poverty. I'll never abandon her.

BACK IN ASSISI, FRANCIS WANTED MORE TIME ALONE TO PRAY. ONE DAY:

Yuck! A leper!

I'm sorry that I tried to avoid you.

HE WENT TO A NEARBY HOSPICE AND GAVE ALL HIS MONEY TO THE LEPERS.

I'll come back soon. I want to help you as much as I can.

MEANWHILE, FRANCIS WAS STILL SEEKING HIS WAY IN LIFE. ONE DAY HE WENT TO PRAY IN THE LITTLE CHURCH OF SAN DAMIANO. IT WAS OLD AND RUN-DOWN. THERE, HE HEARD CHRIST SPEAKING TO HIM.

9

"FRANCIS, REBUILD MY CHURCH. IT'S IN RUINS."

"HOW CAN I DO THAT?" FRANCIS WONDERED. HE NEEDED MONEY TO BUY BUILDING MATERIALS. SO HE TOOK SOME OF THE BEST FABRICS FROM HIS FATHER'S STORE AND TRIED TO SELL THEM.

See! You can't beat the quality of this material. At the price I'm asking, it's a great bargain!

HE ALSO SOLD HIS HORSE.

With this money, I'll be able to repair the church.

That's good, but I don't want any trouble with your father.

PIETRO BERNARDONE WAS ANGRY AND UPSET ABOUT WHAT FRANCIS WAS DOING AT SAN DAMIANO. HE HAD HIS OWN SON LOCKED UP.

Your father is away on a trip. Get out of here now while he's gone.

Don't try to force me, Mom. I'm ready to put up with anything for Christ.

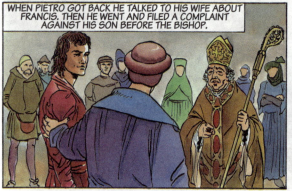

WHEN PIETRO GOT BACK HE TALKED TO HIS WIFE ABOUT FRANCIS. THEN HE WENT AND FILED A COMPLAINT AGAINST HIS SON BEFORE THE BISHOP.

Francis, you can't keep the money you received from selling your father's goods. You have to give it back to him.

FRANCIS SHOCKED EVERYONE BY TAKING OFF ALL HIS CLOTHES;

I'm returning his money and everything else. From now on, I have no father except the one who is in heaven.

FRANCIS WAS FREE. HE LEFT THE CITY AND SANG FOR JOY.

Jesus Christ is my Master and I'm his servant. Praise the Lord!

FOR A WHILE HE WORKED IN THE KITCHEN OF A MONASTERY, THEN IN A HOSPITAL FOR LEPERS. FINALLY HE WENT BACK TO SAN DAMIANO AND BEGAN TO REBUILD THE CHURCH.

God will reward you if you give me a stone.

What do you think you're doing, you idiot!

Be quiet! He's only trying to do some good. I'm happy to give him a stone.

Will you come to help me, too?

AFTER RESTORING SAN DAMIANO, FRANCIS ALSO REPAIRED THE CHAPEL OF ST. MARY OF THE ANGELS. IT WAS IN A VALLEY ABOUT 2 MILES FROM ASSISI.

AROUND THE YEAR 1208 OR 1209, THE GOSPEL READING AT MASS IMPRESSED FRANCIS A LOT.

Jesus said to his disciples: "Go into the towns and villages and say that the kingdom of God is here. Take nothing with you: no money, no wallet, no walking sticks..."

FRANCIS HAD ALREADY BEEN LIVING IN POVERTY. BUT SUDDENLY HE THOUGHT OF HOW HE COULD LIVE THE GOSPEL BETTER.

May God give you his peace! The God of majesty has come among us as our brother. Don't give up hope – God can fill us with joy!

Clare, how are you?

I'm fine. I've found my calling. I want to be like Francis. But I haven't told anyone yet!

LIKE THE YOUNG CLARE OFFREDUCCIO, OTHER PEOPLE IN ASSISI WERE IMPRESSED BY FRANCIS. IN THE NEXT FEW MONTHS, ELEVEN MEN LEFT THEIR FAMILIES AND JOINED THE "POVERELLO."

Come and praise the Creator!

THE BROTHERS DIVIDED THEIR TIME FOR MANY TASKS. THEY PRAYED, WORKED IN THE FIELDS, HELPED THE SICK IN THE HOSPITAL, BEGGED FOR THEIR DAILY BREAD AND LISTENED TO FRANCIS TEACH.

A FEW MONTHS LATER, FRANCIS SENT THE BROTHERS OUT PREACHING, TWO BY TWO.

May the blessing of Jesus Christ go with you, whether you are walking or resting, whether you are awake or asleep, whether you are living or dead.

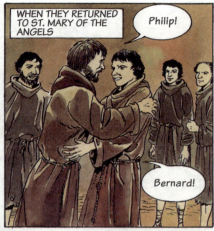

WHEN THEY RETURNED TO ST. MARY OF THE ANGELS

Philip!

Bernard!

See, this angel is a new brother!

Let's have a drink of wine to celebrate your return!

In a dream I saw some great things: our order will spread all over the earth, and many hundreds will come to join us...

IF THEY WERE TO GROW SO MUCH, THEY NEEDED TO HAVE AN OFFICIAL RULE. SO A DOZEN BROTHERS WENT TO ROME. THE BISHOP OF ASSISI KNEW A CARDINAL THERE WHO INTRODUCED THEM TO POPE INNOCENT III.

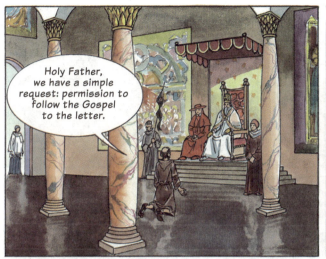

Holy Father, we have a simple request: permission to follow the Gospel to the letter.

I can assure you that they're loyal to the church. They don't belong to any group that's separated from Rome.

Go, my brothers, and live in the way you have said.

HAPPY TO HAVE HIS APPROVAL, THEY PROMISED OBEDIENCE TO THE POPE. THEN THEY RETURNED TO ASSISI.

THEY WENT TO LIVE BY A RIVER NEAR ST. MARY OF THE ANGELS. THEY LIVED IN COMPLETE POVERTY AND IN PRAYER.

Show me your face, O Lord! Day after day I seek your face.

My God, have mercy on me.

In all humility, Lord, I give myself totally to you.

15

THE BEGINNING OF THE YEAR 1212, IN THE HOME OF THE WEALTHY OFFREDUCCIO FAMILY, CLARE'S PARENTS WERE NAGGING HER ABOUT GETTING MARRIED.

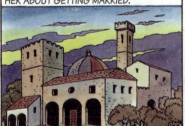

Your father doesn't want you to wait any longer. You're already 16 years old.

Has he already set a date for my wedding? That means I must make a decision.

SHE MADE HER DECISION ON PALM SUNDAY.

The coast is clear. Nobody heard us.

Do you see those lights over there? That's where Brother Francis is going to meet us.

THE "POVERELLO" CUT CLARE'S HAIR AND GAVE HER A ROUGH HABIT LIKE THE ONES THE BROTHERS WORE. CLARE'S PARENTS WERE FURIOUS. THEY BECAME EVEN MORE ANGRY WHEN HER YOUNGER SISTER CATHERINE ALSO JOINED FRANCIS. SHE TOOK THE NAME OF AGNES AS A POOR CLARE. COUNT OFFREDUCCIO CAME TO TAKE HIS DAUGHTERS AWAY.

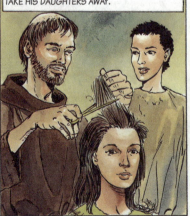

We're not going to leave here. We'd rather die.

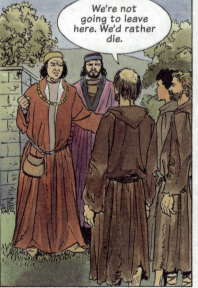

CLARE'S FATHER KNEW HE WAS DEFEATED. THE BISHOP THEN GAVE SAN DAMIANO TO THE SISTERS TO LIVE IN.

16

What a relief! Now we're free to follow the Lord as his poor servants.

FRANCIS LOVED ALL CREATURES. ONE DAY HE WAS OUT WALKING. HE WAS AMAZED TO SUDDENLY FIND HIM- SELF IN THE MIDDLE OF A FLOCK OF BIRDS.

My brothers, the birds, praise the Lord! He's given you everything: freedom to fly, water to drink and trees to nest in. You don't have to make any clothes: he's clothed you with brilliant colors! Don't be ungrateful! Praise the Creator who loves you!

THE BIRDS LISTENED SILENTLY. THEN THEY BEGAN TO WHISTLE AND SING. SUDDENLY THEY BEAT THEIR WINGS AND FLEW OFF IN ALL DIRECTIONS.

MANY PEOPLE WERE ATTRACTED BY THE MESSAGE AND EXAMPLE OF THE "POOR MAN OF ASSISI." AT THE HOUSE OF THE NOBLE ROMAN LADY JACOBA SETTESOLI.

If I could, I'd like to live like Sister Clare and the other poor women.

But you have your two children...

17

But their father left them a lot of money. It's my duty to take care of it for them.

I got the recipe for this almond custard from my husband's family, the Frangipanis*.

This is the best custard I've ever tasted!

I'm very grateful for all of your help. You're truly a faithful friend, "Friar Jacoba."

Don't forget about all the other Christians who would like to follow you too, just as I would. But they aren't able to.

SO FRANCIS WROTE TO ALL THESE PEOPLE. THIS LETTER "TO ALL OF THE FAITHFUL" WAS THE BEGINNING OF THE RULE FOR THE THIRD ORDER FRANCISCANS**.

AROUND THIS TIME, THREE OUTLAWS STARTED TO MAKE TROUBLE IN THE AREA.

We're hungry! Give us something to eat!

You thieves, you murderers, how can you dare to knock at our door?

* THIS BECAME THE NAME OF AN ALMOND CAKE CALLED "FRANGIPANE."
** TODAY THESE LAY FOLLOWERS OF FRANCIS ARE KNOWN AS THE SECULAR FRANCISCAN ORDER.

WHEN FRANCIS CAME BACK HOME, THE BROTHERS TOLD HIM WHAT HAD HAPPENED.

You were rude to them. Jesus wouldn't have treated them that way. Now go find them and give them some food.

FRANCIS WENT TO PRAY AND THE BROTHER WENT OUT LOOKING FOR THE THIEVES.

Please forgive me! I'm sorry for the way I treated you.

THE THIEVES WERE AMAZED AT THIS. THEY WENT BACK TO TALK TO FRANCIS.

Do you think that God can't forgive you? You've committed many crimes...

But God's love is greater than your sins.

THEY BECAME BROTHERS AND BEGAN TO LIVE HOLY LIVES.

EVERY YEAR, THE BROTHERS MET NEAR ST. MARY OF THE ANGELS FOR A SPECIAL MEETING. IN 1217 THEY HAD TWO SPECIAL GUESTS: CARDINAL HUGOLINO, A FUTURE POPE, AND ST. DOMINIC.

Thanks for going out of your way to meet with us.

berzosa

19

Your work is close to my heart. It's the future of the church.

Your joyous poverty gives good example to all Christians. The friars in our Order of Preachers want to do the same.

THEY WERE AMAZED BY WHAT HAPPENED THEN. IT SEEMED THAT NO ONE WAS WORRIED ABOUT FEEDING ALL THE PEOPLE, SUDDENLY:

It's a miracle! Food is coming!

I'm sure that everybody in the area heard about us.

THE MEETING IN 1217 SENT FRIARS TO SYRIA AND TO TUNIS (TO NON-CHRISTIANS). THEN IN 1219 MORE WERE SENT. IN 1219 FRANCIS WENT TO EGYPT AND VISITED THE SULTAN.

Tomorrow we're going to attack the enemy. Brother Francis, pray for us.

Too bad for you! You're going to be defeated. Why shed all the blood for nothing?

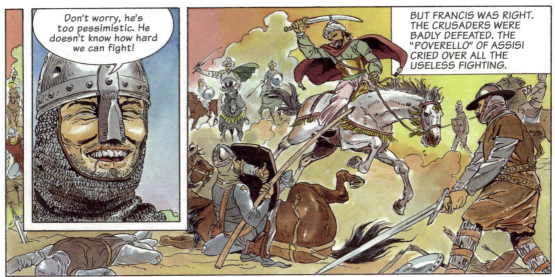

Don't worry, he's too pessimistic. He doesn't know how hard we can fight!

BUT FRANCIS WAS RIGHT. THE CRUSADERS WERE BADLY DEFEATED. THE "POVERELLO" OF ASSISI CRIED OVER ALL THE USELESS FIGHTING.

Where are you going? Are you plotting something?

I want to talk to the sultan and convert him to the Gospel.

You're crazy! The sultan pays people to chop off the heads of Christians!

Oh no!

Don't be afraid! We have nothing to fear if the Lord is with us.

FRANCIS ARRIVED AT THE SARACEN CAMP.

Sultan! Sultan!

Maybe they're negotiators. Take them to the sultan.

21

May God give you peace! Our Savior Jesus Christ endured many sufferings for you.

What you said impressed me, and I admire your courage. Would you like to rest here a little?

I would, on the condition that you and your people convert to Christ.

Allow me to undergo a test by fire. If I die, it will be because of my sins. But if God protects me, promise me that you'll convert to Christ.

There's no point. My people would never accept my conversion to Christianity.

THE SULTAN OFFERED SOME VALUABLE GIFTS TO THE "POVERELLO." BUT FRANCIS ONLY ACCEPTED ONE OF THEM: A HORN WHICH HE PLANNED TO USE TO SIGNAL THE TIME FOR PRAYER.

It's too bad that I haven't been able to convince you. I feel sad about that.

Keep on praying for me anyway. May God show me where the truth lies.

THE KNIGHT OF CHRIST THEN WENT TO THE HOLY LAND.

I praise you Nazareth, blessed city! Your streets and houses hold the memory of our Savior.

IN THE MEANTIME, SOME OF THE BROTHERS CAME FROM ITALY.

Francis, you've got to go back home. Your work is being ruined!

Those who've been in charge while you've been gone have started to build fancy places to live. They also want to build libraries and ask for a lot of donations. They're trying to get rid of your faithful followers.

I have to leave this beautiful country.

THE FOUNDER OF THE ORDER SAILED TO VENICE AND THEN WENT TO BOLOGNA. THERE, THE UPSTARTS HAD OPENED A HOUSE OF STUDIES.

What have you done? Where is poverty, the great love of our order? Leave this house of riches! Shut it down! This is all your fault, and I blame you for it!

INSTEAD OF GOING TO ST. MARY OF THE ANGELS, FRANCIS WENT TO ROME. THE POPE ASKED CARDINAL HUGOLINO TO SETTLE THE MATTER.

The brothers who are responsible for this would never obey me anymore.

What you can do in a small group may not work with a bigger one.

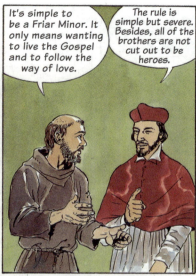

It's simple to be a Friar Minor. It only means wanting to live the Gospel and to follow the way of love.

The rule is simple but severe. Besides, all of the brothers are not cut out to be heroes.

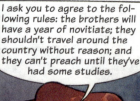

I ask you to agree to the following rules: the brothers will have a year of novitiate; they shouldn't travel around the country without reason; and they can't preach until they've had some studies.

FRANCIS AGREED TO THIS. IN 1221 HE WROTE A NEW RULE WHICH WAS LESS STRICT. IN 1223:

The Pope is coming to give official approval to the rule. Aren't you happy with it?

I no longer find the true Gospel in it.

Brother Leo, God wants us to be poor, humble and to serve everybody... we don't have to do great things.

FOR FRANCIS, THE NEXT TWO YEARS WERE THE MOST DIFFICULT OF HIS LIFE.

My God, my God, why have you abandoned me?

Why do you keep away from us? Don't stay out here in the cold.

I don't want the brothers to see me like this. I feel like all I can do is cry.

My life's work is falling apart. I've become a stranger to my own brothers...

But you know that you're not a stranger to us...

And neither to Sister Clare. You've been neglecting her all this time. She'd love to see you. Why not invite her to dinner?

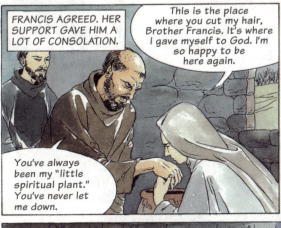

FRANCIS AGREED. HER SUPPORT GAVE HIM A LOT OF CONSOLATION.

This is the place where you cut my hair, Brother Francis. It's where I gave myself to God. I'm so happy to be here again.

You've always been my "little spiritual plant." You've never let me down.

Father, don't give up hope. God never abandons those who give their lives to him.

God, the creator of the stars, lowered himself to become like the least of us.

THE "POVERELLO" SPOKE WITH SO MUCH ENTHUSIASM THAT THEY FORGOT ALL ABOUT EATING.

FRANCIS ESPECIALLY LOVED CHRISTMAS. IN THE YEAR 1223, HE DECIDED TO CELEBRATE IT IN A SPECIAL WAY. HE WAS STAYING IN GRECCIO, NEAR A PLACE WHICH HAD MANY CAVES.

My friend, we want to set up a stable like there was at the first Christmas. The son of God wanted to be born in poverty. How much we can learn from him!

Nobody's thought of that before. What a great idea! I'll get everything ready right away.

ON THE EVENING OF DECEMBER 24

Glory to God! Peace to all people! The joy of heaven has come to earth!

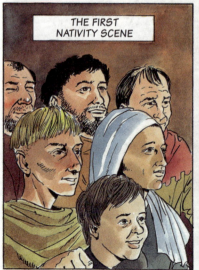

THE FIRST NATIVITY SCENE

FRANCIS SPENT THE WINTER IN GRECCIO. THEN HE WENT TO VISIT THE MINISTER GENERAL*.

* THIS SUCCESSOR OF FRANCIS WAS NOW HEAD OF THE ORDER.

The superior expects others to wait on him, and the brothers have slipped into an easy life. May God pardon them!

ON EASTER DAY, THE "POVERELLO" DECIDED TO TEACH THEM A LESSON.

Give alms to a poor pilgrim for the love of God.

Your meals are too rich for the poor who have to beg for their food. I'll stay here in this corner, which better suits a true Friar Minor.

BUT THE FOUNDER OF THE ORDER WAS NO LONGER IN CHARGE. IN AUGUST, 1224, HE WENT TO MOUNT ALVERNIA*. ONLY HIS CLOSEST FRIENDS WENT WITH HIM.

I sense that I'm going to die soon. I'll stay here. I want to always be faithful to the spirit of poverty. As far as I'm concerned...

* ABOUT 62 MILES NORTHWEST OF ASSISI.

Leave me alone to think. I only want to see Brother Leo.

FRANCIS FASTED FOR A MONTH AND GOD'S PRESENCE CAME NEAR.

My dear Lord, who are you? And who am I, your unworthy servant?

HERE, IN SEPTEMBER 1224, FRANCIS RECEIVED CHRIST'S WOUNDS ON HIS HANDS, FEET AND SIDES.

AFTER RECEIVING THE MARKS OF CHRIST, FRANCIS DECIDED TO GO OUT AND PREACH AGAIN. HE STARTED TO TRAVEL TOWARD GUBBIO.

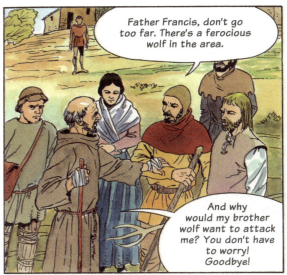

Father Francis, don't go too far. There's a ferocious wolf in the area.

And why would my brother wolf want to attack me? You don't have to worry! Goodbye!

SO FRANCIS WENT TO SEE THE WOLF. HE WASN'T AFRAID.

Come over here, brother wolf! In the name of Jesus Christ, I command you to be gentle.

I've come to take away the bad things which cause you trouble. But you have to live in peace. Do you promise that you won't attack anyone, either people or other animals?

THEN THE WOLF FOLLOWED FRANCIS INTO THE TOWN.

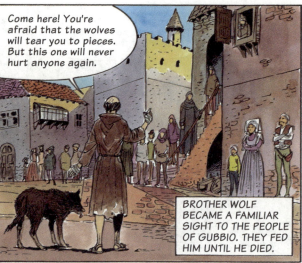

Come here! You're afraid that the wolves will tear you to pieces. But this one will never hurt anyone again.

BROTHER WOLF BECAME A FAMILIAR SIGHT TO THE PEOPLE OF GUBBIO. THEY FED HIM UNTIL HE DIED.

THE "POVERELLO" WAS NOW VERY WEAK AND ALMOST BLIND. BUT HE WANTED TO GO AND VISIT SISTER CLARE AT SAN DAMIANO. THERE HE WROTE HIS MOST BEAUTIFUL HYMN.

Praise be to you, my Lord, for those who forgive others out of love for you, and for those who spread peace.

Praise be to you, my Lord, for our sister bodily death, from which no one can escape.

Praise be to you, my Lord, for all your creatures, especially for my brother the sun. Through him you light up the day, and through him you give us light. Praise be to you, my Lord, for my sister water. She is useful, humble, precious and pure. Praise be to you, my Lord, for my brother fire. Through him you give us light at night. He is handsome, cheerful, brave and strong.

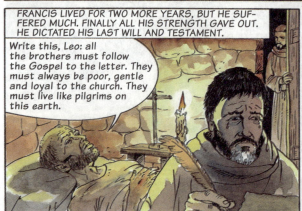

FRANCIS LIVED FOR TWO MORE YEARS, BUT HE SUFFERED MUCH. FINALLY ALL HIS STRENGTH GAVE OUT. HE DICTATED HIS LAST WILL AND TESTAMENT.

Write this, Leo: all the brothers must follow the Gospel to the letter. They must always be poor, gentle and loyal to the church. They must live like pilgrims on this earth.

IN HIS LAST FEW DAYS, HIS SUFFERINGS GOT WORSE. BUT HE CONTINUED TO BLESS THE CITY, THE FRIARS AND THE SISTERS, AND TO PRAISE HIS CREATOR.

Sing for the last time the hymn to the sun!

"Friar Jacoba", I wanted to write to you. As always, you knew what I desired.

SHE WAS CARRYING A BURIAL CLOTH... AND SOME ALMOND CUSTARD. BUT...

I greet you, my sister death, for you lead me to life!

AT THE MOMENT WHEN HE DREW HIS LAST BREATH, A FLOCK OF BIRDS FLEW INTO THE HOUSE. THE BODY OF FRANCIS WAS TAKEN TO ASSISI ON THE NEXT DAY, OCTOBER 4, 1226. THE FUNERAL PROCESSION STOPPED AT SAN DAMIANO.

Francis, my brother, my father, my support! May God glorify you!

TWO YEARS LATER, FRANCIS WAS CANONIZED.

Publishers:

© 2008 - ÉDITIONS DU SIGNE

1, rue Alfred Kastler- Eckbolsheim

B.P. 94 – 67038 Strasbourg, Cedex 2, France

Tel : ++33 (03) 88 78 91 91

Fax : ++33 (03) 88 78 91 99

www.editionsdusigne.fr

email : info@editionsdusigne.fr

ST. ANTHONY MESSENGER PRESS
Cincinnati, Ohio

© 2008 - ST. ANTHONY MESSENGER PRESS

28 W. Liberty Street

Cincinnati, OH 45202

Phone : 513-241-5615

Fax : 513-241-1197

www.AmericanCatholic.org

Printed in Singapore